Dedication

This book is dedicated to
educators across the world
who have the love and passion
to teach! Your dedication
absolutely shapes and
influences the world!

Thank you...

Encouragement for EDUCATORS

Encouragement

For

EDUCATORS

Inspirational Quotes for Good Days and
Those Not So Good Days

CURT THOMAS

www.CurtThomasSpeaks.com

Encouragement for EDUCATORS

ISBN: 978-0-9961977-1-7

Library of Congress Control Number: 2015904058

CURT THOMAS UNLIMITED, LLC Orangeburg, SC

www.CurtThomasSpeaks.com

<u>USE</u>

This quotes book is designed to be inspirational and motivational for the reader.

It is designed for you to read and re-read from time to time.

The hope of the author is for your consciousness to grow to reveal a different interpretation each time you read a quote in this book. Whether it's every day or once a week, motivation and inspiration is continual.

Encouragement for EDUCATORS

<u>Quotes</u>

Encouragement for EDUCATORS

"It is the supreme art of the teacher to awaken joy in creative expression and knowledge."

~Albert Einstein

"I like a teacher who gives you something to take home to think about besides homework."

~Lily Tomlin

"The dream begins with a teacher who believes in you, who tugs and pushes and leads you to the next plateau, sometimes poking you with a sharp stick called 'truth.'"

~Dan Rather

"In teaching you cannot see the fruit of a day's work. It is invisible and remains so, maybe for twenty years."

~Jacques Barzun

"Teaching creates
all other
professions."

~Author Unknown

"What we want is to see the child in pursuit of knowledge, and not knowledge in pursuit of the child."

~George Bernard Shaw

"I cannot teach
anybody anything,
I can only make
them think."

~Socrates

"If you are planning for a year, sow rice; if you are planning for a decade, plant trees; if you are planning for a lifetime, educate people."

~Chinese Proverb

"A teacher is one who makes himself progressively unnecessary."

~Thomas Carruthers

"Good teaching is one-fourth preparation and three-fourths theater."

~Gail Godwin

"A teacher who is attempting to teach without inspiring the pupil with a desire to learn is hammering on cold iron."

~Horace Mann

"Teach the children so it will not be necessary to teach the adults."

~Abraham Lincoln

"A teacher affects eternity; he can never tell where his influence stops."

~Henry Brooks Adams

"A good teacher is like a candle — it consumes itself to light the way for others."

~Mustafa Kemal Atatürk, translated from Turkish

"If you have knowledge, let others light their candles at it."

~Margaret Fuller

"Tell me and I forget. Teach me and I remember. Involve me and I learn."

~Benjamin Franklin"

"A good teacher is a master of simplification and an enemy of simplism."

~Louis A. Berman

"Education is not preparation for life; education is life" itself."

~John Dewey

"Good teachers are costly, but bad teachers cost more."

~Bob Talbert

"The mediocre teacher tells. The good teacher explains. The superior teacher demonstrates. The great teacher inspires."

~William Arthur Ward

"The best teacher is the one who suggests rather than dogmatizes, and inspires his listener with the wish to teach himself."

~Edward Bulwer-Lytton

"A teacher's purpose is not to create students in his own image, but to develop students who can create their own image."

~Author Unknown

"What the teacher is,
is more important
than what he
teaches."

~Karl Menninger

"Teaching should be
full of ideas instead
of stuffed with
facts."

~Author Unknown

"A mind when stretched by a new idea never regains its original dimensions."

~Anonymous

"Teaching is leaving a vestige of one self in the development of another. And surely the student is a bank where you can deposit your most precious treasures."

~Eugene P. Bertin

"Teachers who inspire know that teaching is like cultivating a garden, and those who would have nothing to do with thorns must never attempt to gather flowers."

~Author Unknown

"Teachers who inspire realize there will always be rocks in the road ahead of us. They will be stumbling blocks or stepping stones; it all depends on how we use them."

~Author Unknown

"Teaching is not a lost art, but the regard for it is a lost tradition."

~Jacques Barzun

"The best way to predict your future is to create it."

~Abraham Lincoln

"A teacher's job is to take a bunch of live wires and see that they are well-grounded."

~D. Martin

"What a teacher writes on the blackboard of life can never be erased."

~Author Unknown

"The teacher who is indeed wise does not bid you to enter the house of his wisdom but rather leads you to the threshold of your mind."

~Khalil Gibran

"Discover wildlife: be a teacher!"

~Author Unknown

"Children must be
taught how to think,
not what to think."

~Margaret Mead

"When you teach your son, you teach your son's son."

~ The Talmud

"The best teachers teach from the heart, not from the book."

~Author Unknown

"The average teacher explains complexity; the gifted teacher reveals simplicity."

~Robert Brault

"Often, when I am reading a good book, I stop and thank my teacher. That is, I used to, until she got an unlisted number."

~Author Unknown

"2 Teach is
2 Touch lives
4 Ever"

~Author Unknown

"Who dares to teach must never cease to learn."

~John Cotton Dana

"There are three good reasons to be a teacher — June, July, and August."

~Author Unknown

"A truly special teacher is very wise, and sees tomorrow in every child's eyes."

~Author Unknown

"A teacher should have maximal authority, and minimal power."

~Thomas Szasz

"To teach is to learn twice."

~Joseph Joubert

"The secret of teaching is to appear to have known all your life what you just learned this morning."

~Author Unknown

"Teachers touch the future."

~Author Unknown

"Don't try to fix the students, fix ourselves first. The good teacher makes the poor student good and the good student superior. When our students fail, we, as teachers, too, have failed."

~Marva Collins

"The object of teaching a child is to enable him to get along without his teacher."

~Elbert Hubbard

"Teaching is the only major occupation of man for which we have not yet developed tools that make an average person capable of competence and performance. In teaching we rely on the "naturals," the ones who somehow know how to teach."

~Peter Drucker

"Teachers are expected to reach unattainable goals with inadequate tools. The miracle is that at times they accomplish this impossible task."

~Haim G. Ginott

"The art of teaching is the art of assisting discovery."

~Mark Van Doren

"If you promise not to believe everything your child says happens at school, I'll promise not to believe everything he says happens at home."

~Anonymous Teacher

"The secret in education lies in respecting the student."

~Ralph Waldo Emerson

"Education is what survives when what has been learned has been forgotten."

~B.F. Skinner

"When you learn, teach. When you get, give."

~Maya Angelou

"A child mis-educated
is a child lost."

~John F. Kennedy

"I am not a teacher,
but an awakener."

~Robert Frost

"Don't just teach your kids to read, teach them to question what they read. Teach them to question everything!"

~George Carlin

"Live as if you were to die tomorrow. Learn as if you were to live forever."

~Mahatma Gandhi

"What we learn with pleasure we never forget."

~Alfred Mercier

"The beautiful thing about learning is that no one can take it away from you."

~B.B. King

"Better than a thousand days of diligent study is one day with a great teacher."

~Japanese Proverb

"Logic will get you from A to B. Imagination will take you everywhere."

~Albert Einstein

"Education is the most powerful weapon which you can use to change the world."

~Nelson Mandela

"The hardest thing to teach is how to care."

~Unknown

"Laughter is timeless. Imagination has no age. And dreams are forever."

~Walt Disney

"Each of us has a fire in our hearts for something. It's our goal in life to find it and keep it lit."

~Mary Lou Retton

"Plant your own garden and decorate your own soul, instead of waiting for someone to bring you flowers."

~Veronica A. Shoffstall

"The more that you read, the more things you will know, the more that you learn, the more places you'll go."

~Dr. Seuss

"Do not confine your children to your own learning, for they were born in another time."

~Chinese Proverb

"Tell me and I forget, teach me and I may remember, involve me and I learn."

~Benjamin Franklin

"I never respected my 9th grade teacher until I got my report card at the end of the semester. Respect indeed!"

~Curt Thomas

"Teachers can change lives with just the right mix of chalk and challenges."

~Joyce Meyer

"You can get help from teachers, but you are going to have to learn a lot by yourself, sitting alone in a room."

~Dr. Seuss

"Most of us end up with no more than five or six people who remember us. Teachers have thousands of people who remember them for the rest of their lives."

~Andy Rooney

"You can have great teachers, but if you don't have a good principal, you won't have a good school."

~Eli Broad

"My mom was a teacher - I have the greatest respect for the profession - we need great teachers - not poor or mediocre ones."

~Condoleezza Rice

"If you have to put someone on a pedestal, put teachers. They are society's heroes."

~Guy Kawasaki

"I was lucky that I met the right mentors and teachers at the right moment."

~James Levine

"A teacher affects eternity; he can never tell where his influence stops."

~Henry Brooks Adams

"A teacher is one who makes himself progressively unnecessary."

~Thomas Carruthers

"I like a teacher who gives you something to take home to think about besides homework."

~Lily Tomlin

"Man's mind stretched by a new idea never goes back to its original dimensions."

~Oliver Wendell Holmes

"Teaching is the profession that teaches all the other professions."

~Author Unknown

"Teaching kids to count is fine, but teaching them what counts is best."

~Bob Talbert

"Education is the
mother of leadership."

~Wendell L. Willkie

"We learn by
teaching."

~James Howell

"The art of teaching is the art of assisting discovery."

~Mark van Doren

"Education is the best provision for old age."

~Aristotle

"Every truth has four corners: as a teacher I give you one corner, and it is for you to find the other three."

~Confucius

"Optimism is the faith that leads to achievement, nothing can be done without hope and confidence."

~Helen Keller

"Treat people as if they were what they ought to be and you help them become what they are capable of becoming."

~Goethe

"It is not what is poured into a student that counts but what is planted."

~Linda Conway

"Education is not the filling of a pail but the lighting of a fire."

~William Butler Yeats

"The job of an educator is to teach students to see the vitality in themselves."

~Joseph Campbell

"The greatest sign of success for a teacher ... is to be able to say, 'The children are now working as if I did not exist.'"

~Maria Montessori

"Teaching kids to count is fine, but teaching them what counts is best."

~Bob Talber

"Everybody is a genius. But if you judge a fish by its ability to climb a tree it will live its whole life believing that it is stupid."

~Anonymous

"My teacher gave me a reason to believe again after I failed made in the 9th grade. He simply made math fun!"

~Curt Thomas

"Good teaching is more a giving of right questions than a giving of right answers."

~Josef Albers

"Teacher : The child's third parent."

~Hyman Berston

"The best teachers
teach from the heart,
not from the book."

~Author Unknown

"He who opens a school door, closes a prison."

~Victor Hugo

"A gifted teacher is as rare as a gifted doctor, and makes far less money."

~Author Unknown

"The mediocre teacher tells. The good teacher explains. The superior teacher demonstrates. The great teacher inspires."

~William Arthur Ward

Thank you for all that you do. It's because of educators like you, we are...

-Curt

<u>Like us on Facebook:</u>

<u>Keyword:</u> Curt Thomas Motivational Speaker

<u>Instagram:</u>

<u>Keyword:</u> @CurtThomasSpeaks

<u>Follow on Twitter:</u>

<u>Keyword:</u> @CurtSpeaks

www.ingramcontent.com/pod-product-compliance
Lightning Source LLC
Chambersburg PA
CBHW070813050426
42452CB00011B/2023